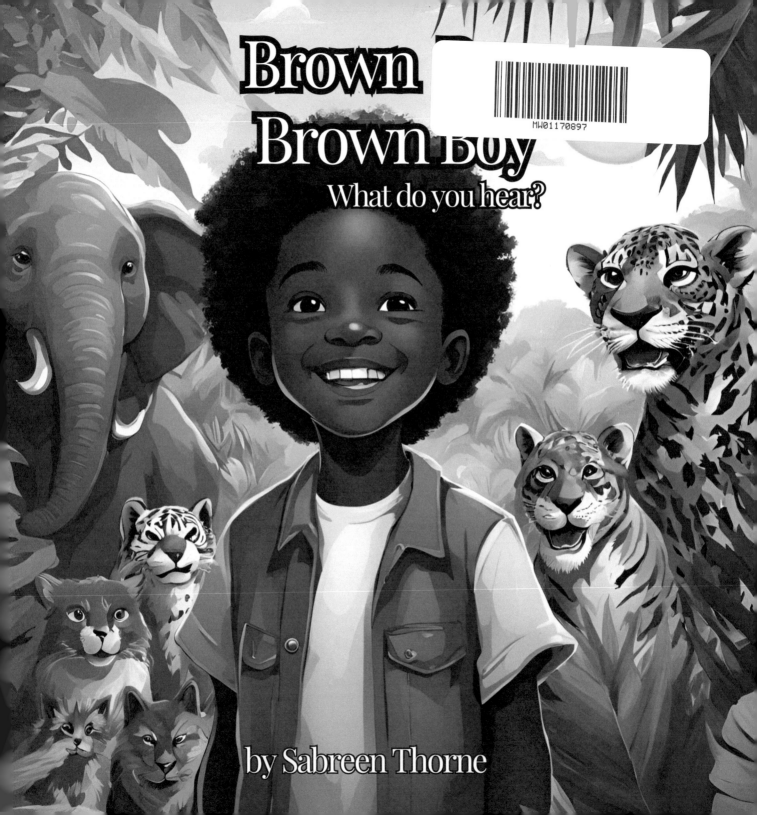

Brown Brown Boy

What do you hear?

by Sabreen Thorne

This book belongs to

_____

Published by Amazon KDP, July 2024
ISBN: 9798333027214

Illustrations created using AI software on Canva.

Summary: An African American boy hears a variety of jungle animals, each one a different sound or tone, and the boy's father appears at the end, who the boy has been learning from.

For permission requests, write to the author at sabreenthorne@gmail.com
First Edition

To my bonus son, *Ja'Khristian* my fearless & inquisitive *brown boy.*

– ST

"I hear an elephant trumpeting in my ear."

"I hear a lion roaring in my ear."

"I hear a snake hissing in my ear."

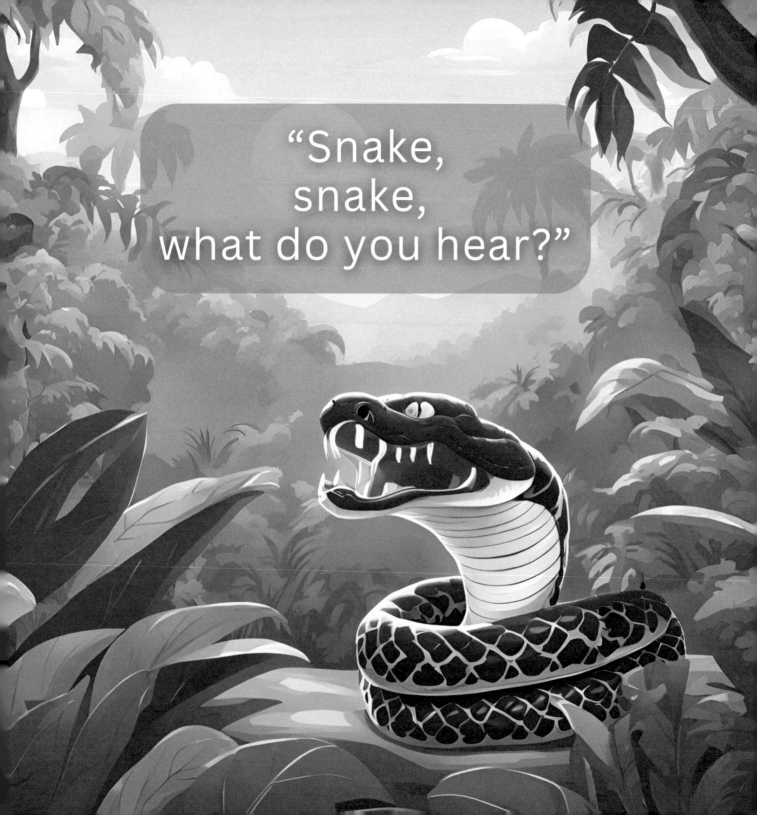

"I hear a hyena laughing in my ear."

"I hear a parrot mimicking other animals and whistling in my ear."

"I hear a jaguar growling in my ear."

"I hear a chimpanzee panting and hooting in my ear."

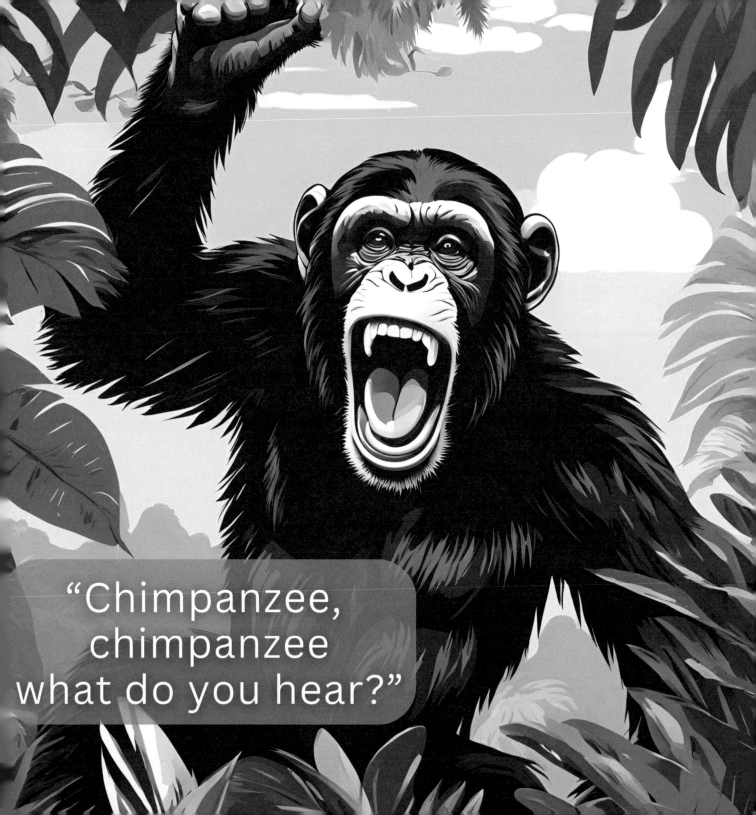

"I hear a gorilla thumping and grunting in my ear."

"I hear a toucan yelping and screeching in my ear."

"I hear a tiger roaring and growling in my ear."

"I hear a brown man talking in my ear."

"I hear a brown boy asking questions in my ear."

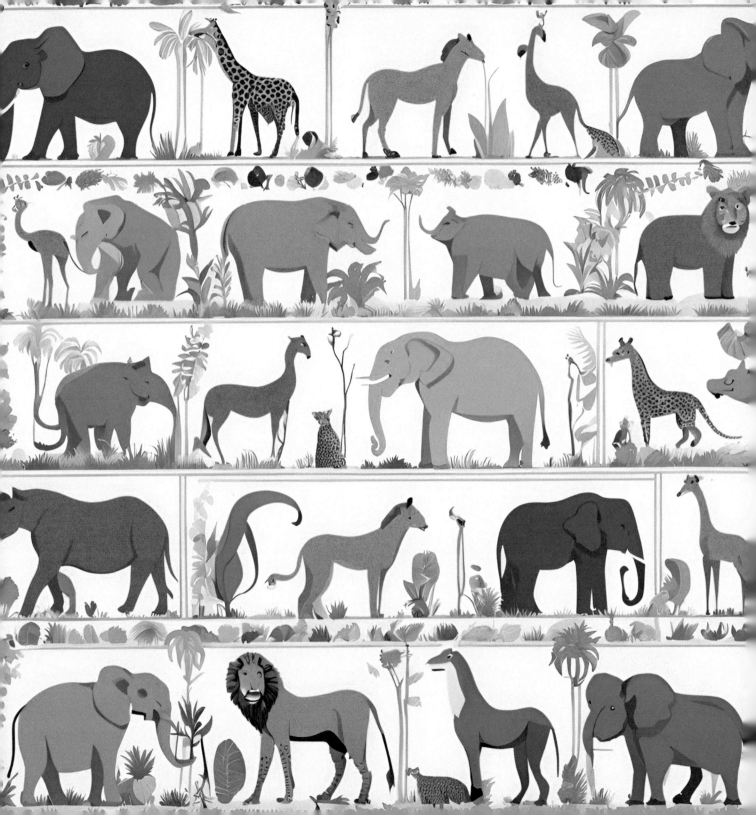

Made in the USA
Columbia, SC
19 November 2024

46761448R00020